The Two Boats of Herakles

Poems by Matt Bodett

Printed in the United States of America

First Printing, 2020

ISBN: 978-1-7347545-4-4

Press Here
410 S Michigan Ave Suite 420
Chicago, IL 60605

www.mattbodett.com

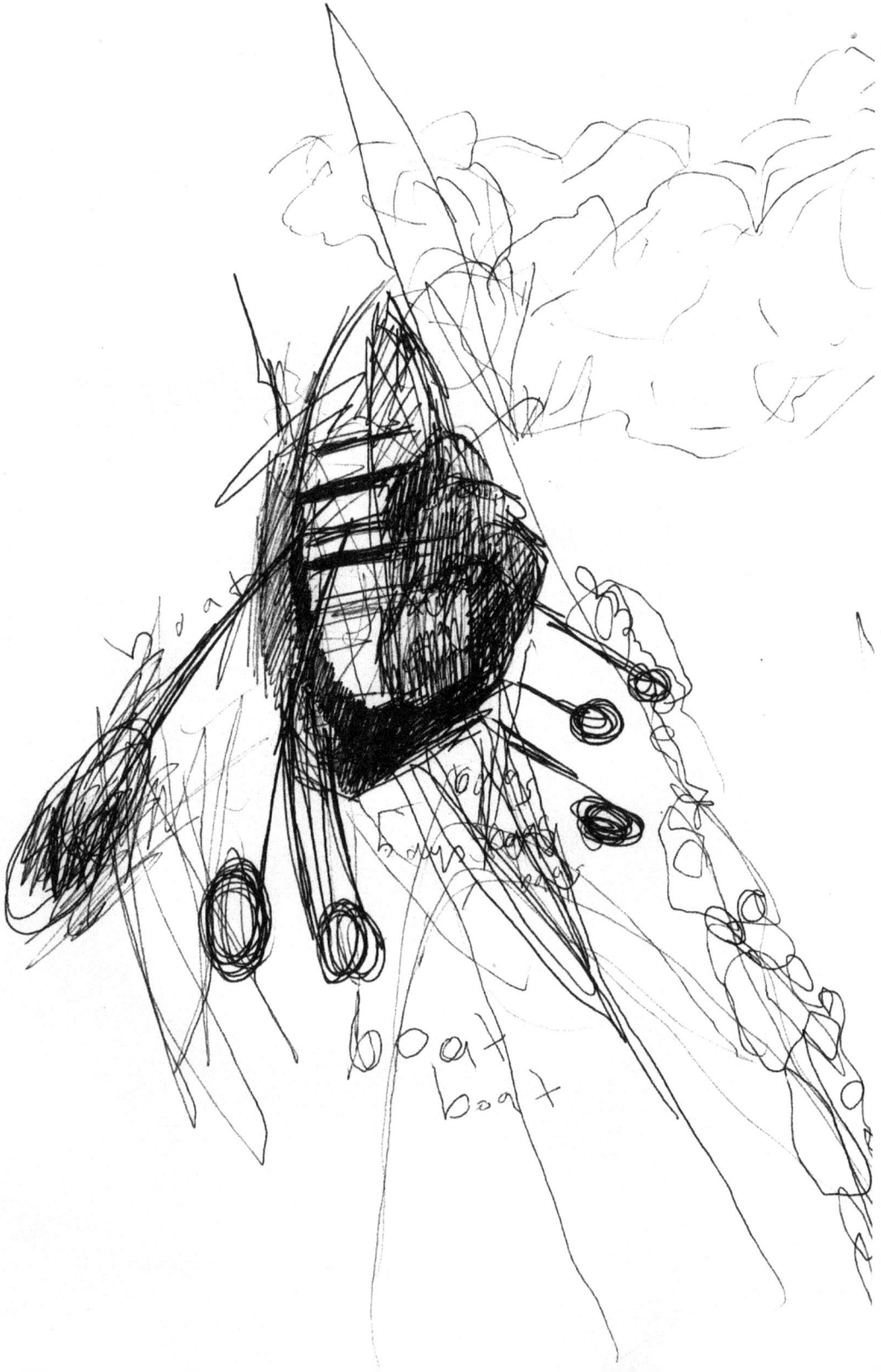

boat

boat

boat

Recite the alphabet.

Count from 1 to 50.

Name the months.

What is the largest river in America?

Who is the ruler of England?

What is twelve times thirteen?

Can you tell me, please, your full name?

Name_____ Date_____

Date of Birth_____ Phone Number_____

Primarry Care Physician_____

Do you give permission for ongoing regular updates to be
provided to you Primary Care Physician? ☐ Yes ☐ No

Current Therapist/Counselor_____

Therapist's Phone Number_____

Please indicate which symptoms occur more often than you would
like them to:

☐ Anger/agression
☐ Antisocial behavior
☐ Avoiding people
☐ Cyber addiction
☐ Disorientation/Dizziness
☐ Drug dependence
☐ Eating disorder
☐ Fatigue
☐ Hallucinations
☐ Impulsivity
☐ Judgement errors
☐ Memory impairment
☐ Phobias/fears
☐ Disorganized thoughts
☐ Sexual addiction
☐ Sleeping problems
☐ Trembling
☐ Other (specify)_____

☐ Alcohol dependence
☐ Anxiety/Panic attacks
☐ Chest pain/Heart palpitations
☐ Depression
☐ Distractability
☐ Excessive energy
☐ Elevated Mood
☐ Gambling
☐ High blood pressure
☐ Irritability
☐ Loneliness/withdrawing
☐ Mood shift
☐ Recurring thoughts
☐ Sexual difficulties
☐ Sick often
☐ Suicidal thoughts
☐ Worrying/hopelessness

Breifly describe how the above symptoms impair your ability to
function effectively:_____
_____
_____

Suicide Risk Assessment

Have you ever had feelings or thoughts that you didn't want to live? ☐ Yes ☐ No

If YES, please answer the following. If NO, please skip to the next section.

Do you currently feel that you don't want to live?

How often do you have these thoughts?_____

_____

When was the last time you had thoughts of dying?_____

Has anything happened to make you feel that way?_____

_____

On a scale of 1 to 10 (ten being strongest) how strong is your desire to kill yourself currently?_____

Would anything make it better?_____

_____

Have you ever thought about how you would kill yourself?_____

_____

Is the method you would use readily available?_____

Have you planned a time for this?_____

Is there anything that would stop you from killing yourself?_____

_____

Do you feel hopeless and/or worthless?_____

Have you ever tried to kill or harm yourself before?_____

_____

Do you have access to guns? If yes, please explain_____

_____

Past Medical History:

Allergies_____Current Weight_____

List ALL current prescription medications and how often you take them:
(if none, write none)

Medication Name	Total Daily Dosage	Estimated Start Date

Current over-the-counter medications or supplements:_____

Current medical problems:_____

Past medical problems, nonpsychotic hospitalization, or surgeries:
_____
Have you ever had an EKG? ☐ Yes ☐ No
Was the EKG ☐ normal ☐ abnormal ☐ unknown

For Women only: Date of last menstrual period_____
Are you currently pregnant or do you think you might be pregnant?
☐ Yes ☐ No
Are you planning to get pregnant in the near future? ☐ Yes ☐ No
Birth control method_____
How many times have you been pregnant?_____
How many live births?_____
Do you have any concerns about your physical health that you
would like to discuss?_____

Date and place of last physical exam:_____

Family Information:

Relationship   Name   Age   Living   Living with you

Mother

Father

Brother

Sister

Spouse

Children

Children

Other (specify)

Personal and Family Medical History:

	You	Family	Which Family Member
Thyroid Disease	☐	☐	
Anemia	☐	☐	
Liver Disease	☐	☐	
Chronic Fatigue	☐	☐	
Kidney Disease	☐	☐	
Diabetes	☐	☐	
Asthma/Respiratory	☐	☐	
Stomach or Intestinal	☐	☐	
Cancer (type)	☐	☐	
Fibromyalgia	☐	☐	
Heart Disease	☐	☐	
Epilepsy or Seizures	☐	☐	
Chronic Pain	☐	☐	
High Cholesterol	☐	☐	
High Blood Pressure	☐	☐	
Head Trauma	☐	☐	
Liver Problems	☐	☐	
Other	☐	☐	

Is there any additional personal or family medical history?
☐ Yes ☐ No   If yes, please explain:

When your mother was pregnant with you, were there any complications during the pregnancy or birth?_____

_____

Past Psychiatric History:

Outpatient treatment ☐ Yes ☐ No   If yes, please describe when, by whom, and nature of treatment.

Reason	Dates Treated	By whom

Psychiatric Hospitalization ☐ Yes ☑ No   If yes, describe for what reason, when, and where.

Reason	Date Hospitalized	Where

Past Psychiatric Medications: If you have ever taken any of the following medications, please indicate the dates, dosage, and how helpful they were (if you can't remember all the details, just write in what you do remember).

	Dates	Dosage	Response/Side-Effects
Antidepressants			
Prozac (fluoxetine)			
Zoloft (sertraline)			
Luvox (fluvoxamine)			
Paxil (paroxetine)			
Celexa (citalopram)			
Lexapro (escitalopram)			
Effexor (venlafaxine)			
Cymbalta (duloxetine)			
Wellbutrin (bupropion)			
Remeron (mirtazapine)			
Serzone (nefazodone)			
Anafranil (clomipramine)			
Pamelor (nortrptyline)			

Tofranil (imipramine) _____
Elavil (amitriptyline) _____
Other _____

Mood Stabilizers

	Dates	Dosage	Response/Side-Effects
Tegretol (carbamazepine)			
Lithium			
Depakote (valproate)			
Lamictal (lamotrigine)			
Tegretol (carbamazepine)			
Topamax (topiramate)			
Other			

Antipsychotics/Mood Stabilizers

	Dates	Dosage	Response/Side-Effects
Seroquel (quetiapine)			
Zyprexa (olanzepine)			
Geodon (ziprasidone)			
Abilify (aripiprazole)			
Clozaril (clozapine)			
Haldol (haloperidol)			
Prolixin (fluphenazine)			
Risperdal (risperidone)			
Other			

Sedative/Hypnotics

	Dates	Dosage	Response/Side-Effects
Ambien (zolpidem)			
Sonata (zaleplon)			
Rozerem (ramelteon)			
Restoril (temazepam)			
Desyrel (trazodone)			
Other			

ADHD medications

	Dates	Dosage	Response/Side-Effects
Adderall (amphetamine)			
Concerta (methylphenidate)			
Ritalin (methylphenidate)			

	Dosage	Response/Side-Effects
Strattera (atomoxetine)		
Other		

Antianxiety medications

	Dates	Dosage	Response/Side-Effects
Xanax (alprazolam)			
Ativan (lorazepam)			
Klonopin (clonazepam)			
Valium (diazepam)			
Tranxene (clorazepate)			
Buspar (buspirone)			
Other			

Your Exercise Level:

Do you exercise regularly? ☐ Yes ☐ No

How many days a week do you get exercise? _____

How much time each day do you exercise? _____

What kind of exercise do you do? _____

Familiy Psychiatric History:

Has anyone in your family been diagnosed with or treated for:

Bipolar disorder ☐ Yes ☐ No

Schizophrenia ☑ Yes ☐ No

Depression ☐ Yes ☑ No

Post-traumatic stress ☐ Yes ☐ No

Anxiety ☐ Yes ☐ No

Alcohol abuse ☐ Yes ☐ No

Anger ☐ Yes ☐ No

Other substance abuse ☐ Yes ☐ No

Suicide ☐ Yes ☐ No

Violence ☐ Yes ☐ No

If yes, who had each problem? _____

_____

Has any family member been treated with a psychiatric medica-
tion? ☐ Yes ☐ No If yes, who was treated, what
medications did they take, and how effective was the treatment?

_____

Substance Use:

Have you ever been treated for alcohol or drug use or abuse?
☒ Yes ☐ No

If yes, for which substances? _____

If yes, where were you treated and when? _____

How many days per week do you drink any alcohol? _____

What is the least number of drinks you will drink in a day? _____

What is the most number of drinks you will drink in a day? _____

In the past three months, what is the largest amount of alcoholic drinks you have consumed in one day? _____

Have you ever felt you ought to cut down on your drinking or drug use? ☐ Yes ☐ No

Have people annoyed you by criticizing your drinking or drug use?
☐ Yes ☐ No

Have you ever felt bad or guilty about your drinking or drug use?
☒ Yes ☐ No

Have you ever had a drink or used drugs first thing in the morning to steady your nerves or to get rid of a hangover?
☐ Yes ☐ No

Do you think you may have a problem with alcohol or drug use?
☒ Yes ☐ No

Have you used any street drugs in the past 3 months? ☒ Yes ☐ No

If yes, which ones? _____

Have you ever abused prescription medication? ☐ Yes ☐ No

If yes, which ones and for how long? _____

_____

_____

_____

Check if you have ever tried the following:

	Yes	No
Methamphetamine	☐	☐
Cocaine	☐	☐
Stimulants (pills)	☐	☐
Heroin	☐	☐
LSD or Hallucinogens	☒	☐
Marijuana	☒	☐
Pain killers (not as prescribed)	☒	☐

Methadone ☐ ☐
Tranquilizer/sleeping pills ☐ ☐
Alcohol ☐ ☐
Ecstasy ☐ ☐
Other _____
How many caffeinated beverages do you drink a day?
Coffee _____ Sodas _____ Tea _____

Tobacco History:

Have you ever smoked cigarettes? ☐ Yes ☐ No
Currently? ☐ Yes ☑ No
How many packs per day on average? _____
How many years? _____
In the past? ☐ Yes ☐ No How many years did you smoke? _____
When did you quit? _____
Pipe, cigars, or chewing tobacco: Currently? ☐ Yes ☑ No
In the past? ☐ Yes ☐ No
What kind? _____
How often per day on average? _____ How many years? _____

Family Background and Childhood History:

Were you adopted? ☐ Yes ☐ No Where did you grow up? _____
_____
List your siblings and their ages: _____
_____
_____
_____
What was your father's occupation? _____
What was your mother's occupation? _____

Did your parents divorce? ☐ Yes ☐ No If so, how old were you
when they divorced? _____
If your parents divorced, who did you live with? _____
_____

Describe your father and your relationship with him: _____

_____

_____

Describe your mother and your relationship with her: _____

_____

_____

How old were you when you left home? _____

Has anyone in your immediate family died? _____

Who and when? _____

_____

Trauma History:

Do you have a history of being abused emotionally, sexually,
physically or by neglect? ☐ Yes ☐ No

Please describe when, where and by whom: _____

_____

_____

Educational History:

Highest Grade Completed? _____ Where? _____

Did you attend college? _____ Where? _____

Major? _____

What is your highest educational level or degree attained? _____

Occupational History:

Are you currently: ☐ Working ☐ Student ☐ Unemployed
☐ Disabled ☐ Retired

How long in present position? _____

What is/was your occupation? _____

Where do you work? _____

Have you ever served in the military? ☐ Yes ☐ No. If so, what branch and when? _____

Honorable discharge ☐ Yes ☐ No. Other type discharge _____

Relationship History and Current Family:

Are you currently: ☐ Married ☐ Partnered ☐ Divorced ☐ Single
☐ Widowed

How long? _____

If not married, are you currently in a relationship? ☐ Yes ☐ No

If yes, how long? _____

Are you sexually active? ☐ Yes ☐ No

How would you identify your Gender? ☐ Male ☐ Female
☐ Transgender ☐ Other ☐ I prefer not to answer

How would you identify your sexual orientation?

☐ straight/heterosexual ☐ lesbian/gay/homosexual ☐ bisexual
☐ transsexual ☐ unsure/questioning ☐ asexual ☐ other
☐ prefer not to answer

What is your spouse or significant other's occupation? _____

_____

Describe your relationship with your spouse or significant other:

_____

_____

Have you had any prior marriages? ☐ Yes ☐ No. If so, how many?

How long? _____

Do you have children? ☐ Yes ☐ No If yes, list ages and gender:
_____
_____

Describe your relationship with your children: _____
_____
_____

List everyone who currently lives with you: _____
_____
_____

Legal History:

Have you ever been arrested? ☐ Yes ☐ No
If yes, when and where? _____
Do you have any pending legal problems? ☐ Yes ☐ No
If yes, please describe and indicate the court and hearing/trial
dates and charges: _____
_____

Are you currently on probation or parole? ☐ Yes ☐ No

Leisure/Recreational:

Describe special areas of interest or hobbies (e.g., art, books,
crafts, physical fitness, sports, outdoor activities, etc.)

Activity	How often?	How often in the past?
_____	_____	_____
_____	_____	_____

Spirituality:

Do you belong to a particular ___ religion ___?

☐ Yes ☐ No

If yes, what is the level of your involvement ___

Do you find your involvement helpful ___ ___ the level ___

of this involvement make things more difficult or

stressful for you? ☐ more helpful ☐ stressful ___

Is there anything else that you would like us to know?

Signature _____ Date _____

Guardian Signature (if under age 18) _____

Date _____

Emergency Contact _____

Telephone # _____

Please indicate which of the following apply to you:

☐ Not being good enough

☐ Not being cared about

☐ Not belonging/fitting in

☐ Being understood

☐ Being rejected

☐ Being abandoned

☐ Being a failure

☐ Being unattractive

☐ Being overweight

☐ Hopelessness

☐ Not knowing my identity

☐ Hearing voices or sounds inside my head

☐ Hearing voices or sounds that others can't or don't hear

☐ Seeing things or people that others can't or don't see

☐ Having special powers

☐ Being superior or privileged

☐ Being in danger

☐ Probelms with stealing

☐ Problems with vandalism

Have you spoken of your visions to anyone else?

- ☐ Problems with fire setting

- ☐ Injuring self

- ☐ Suicidal acts

- ☐ Suicidal thoughts

- ☐ Feeling the need to boss/control others

- ☐ Excess use of drugs/alcohol

- ☐ Excessive gambling

- ☐ Excess sex

- ☐ Child abuse and/or neglect

- ☐ Problems with Spirituality or religion

- ☐ Problems with relationships

- ☐ Financial problems

Do people around you believe you are sent from God?

Have you had or do you have problems with feelings of:

☐ Guilt

☐ Apathy or indifference

☐ Boredom

☐ Intense loneliness

☐ Intense sadness

☐ Helplessness

☐ Depression

☐ Aggression

☐ Irritability

☐ Intense frustration

☐ Anger

☐ Hate

☐ Rage

☐ Tension

☐ Being under a lot of pressure

☐ Being out of control

☐ Anxiety/apprehension

☐ Specific fears/phobias

☐ Intense excitement/euphoria

Are you angry?

- ☐ Obsessive love/infatuation
- ☐ Mistrust/suspiciousness
- ☐ Inefficiency
- ☐ Avoidance
- ☐ Forgetting
- ☐ Lying
- ☐ Impulsiveness
- ☐ Being oppositional
- ☐ Sadistic Acts
- ☐ Attention/concentration
- ☐ Being too dependent
- ☐ Perfectionism
- ☐ Taking the blame
- ☐ Procrastinating
- ☐ Arguing
- ☐ Temper
- ☐ Rebelliousness
- ☐ Self-defeating acts
- ☐ Helping others too much
- ☐ Being taken advantage of

Do the voices counsel you on how to answer these questions?

Will you tell me the truth?

The source materials for this publication come from four sources:

First, the introductory questions come from seventeen standard intellegence questions asked of incoming inmates at the Ionia State Hospital for the Criminally Insane. These questions were found in "Protest Psychosis: How Schizophrenia Became a Black Disease" written by Jonathan M. Metzel.

Second, the questionnaire is a composite of various psychiatric intake forms which I have gathered and condensed into this format.

Third, the final set of questions come from the trial of Joan of Arc as translated by W.S. Scott.

Lastly, the cover, hand written, and hand drawn elements were taken from my personal sketchbook which I utilized while unable to speak during a visit to the hospital for psychiatric care.